20 SHEET MUSIC BESTSELLERS

CHRISTIAN HITS

Arranged by Carol Tornquist

MW00773915

Produced by
Alfred Music Publishing Co., Inc.
P.O. Box 10003
Van Nuys, CA 91410-0003
alfred.com

Printed in USA.

ISBN-10: 0-7390-9128-X
ISBN-13: 978-0-7390-9128-9

Cover photo: Piano keys © iStockphoto.com / Jon Helgason • Grunge background with autumn leaves © iStockphoto.com / javarman3
Power © iStockphoto.com / Kuzma

Alfred Cares. Contents printed on 100% recycled paper.

AMAZING GRACE

(My Chains Are Gone)

Words and Music by
Chris Tomlin and Louie Giglio
Arranged by Carol Tornquist

Moderately slow

with pedal

1. A - maz - ing__ grace! how sweet the sound that

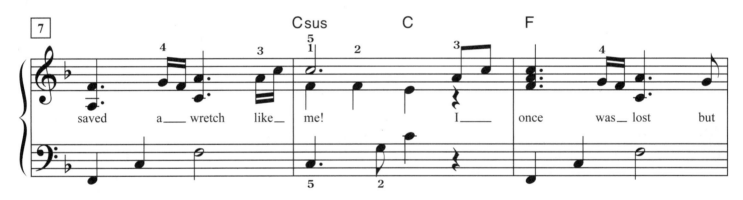

saved a__ wretch like__ me! I__ once was__ lost but

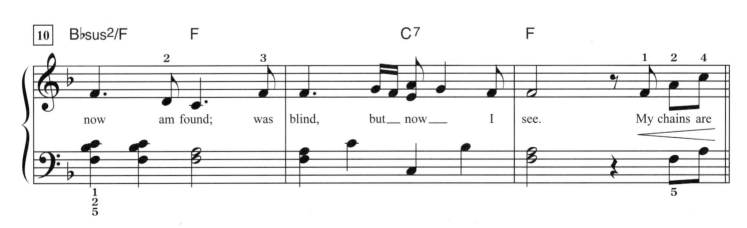

now am found; was blind, but__ now__ I see. My chains are

BLESSINGS

Words and Music by Laura Mixon Story
Arranged by Carol Tornquist

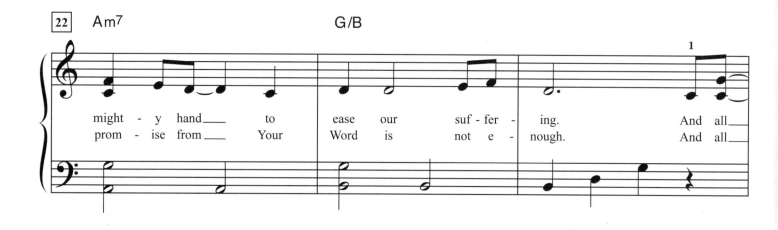

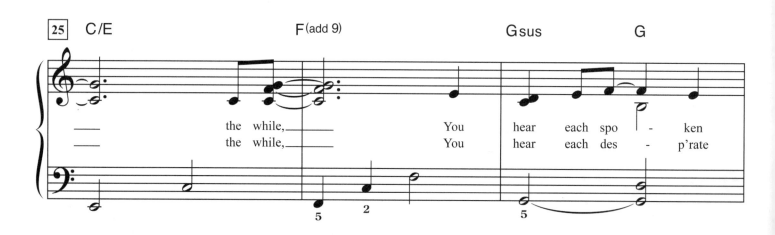

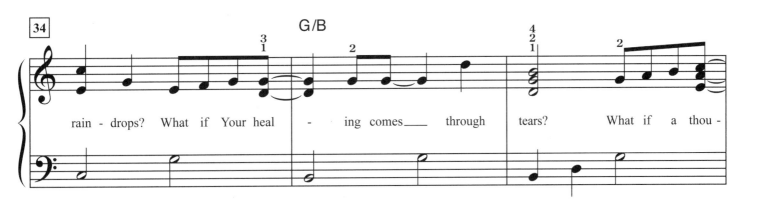

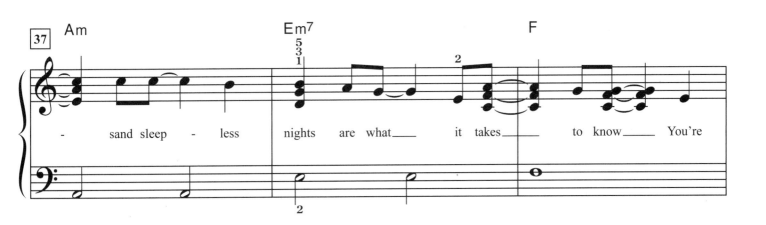

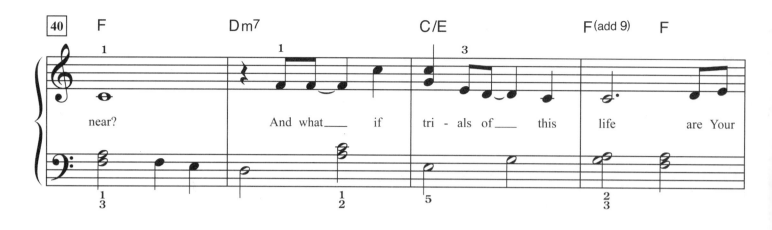

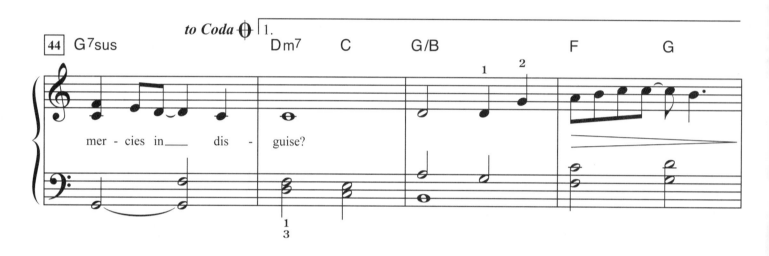

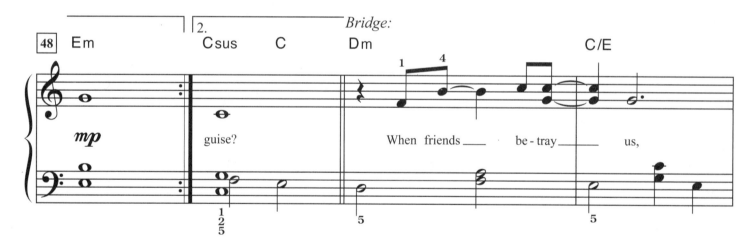

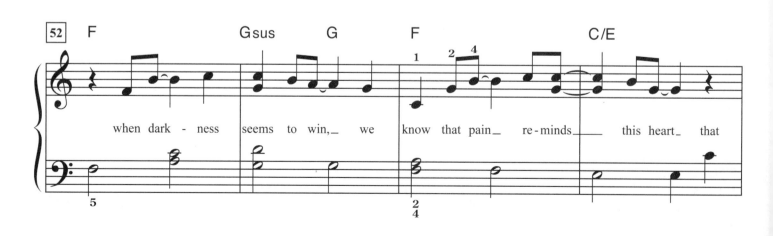

CRY OUT TO JESUS

Words and Music by
Brad Avery, David Carr, Mac Powell, Mark Lee and Tai Anderson
Arranged by Carol Tornquist

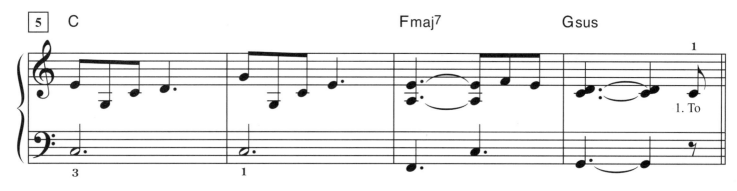

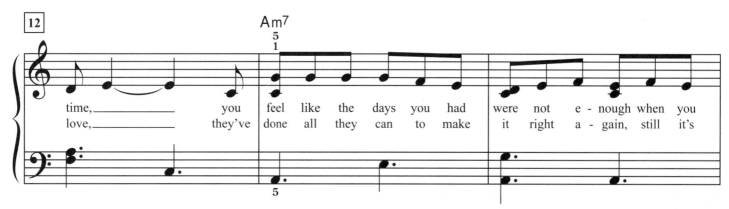

EAST TO WEST

Words and Music by
Bernie Herms and Mark Hall
Arranged by Carol Tornquist

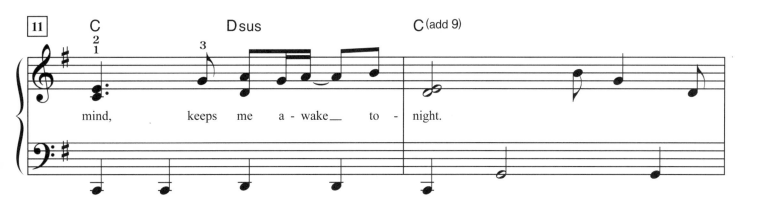

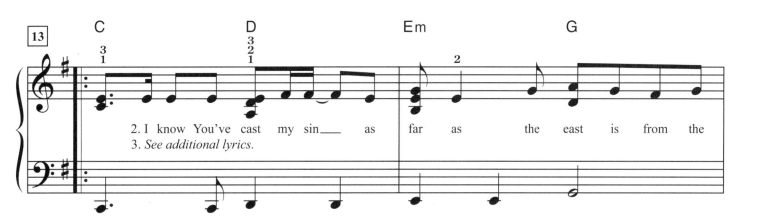

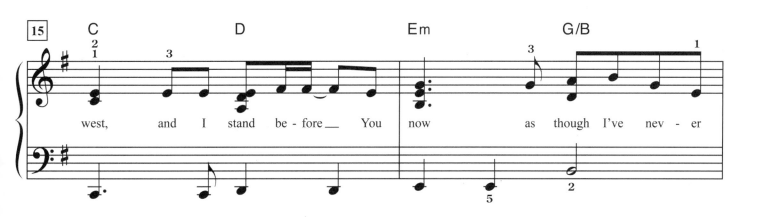

sinned, but to-day I feel like I'm just one mis-take___ a - way from Your

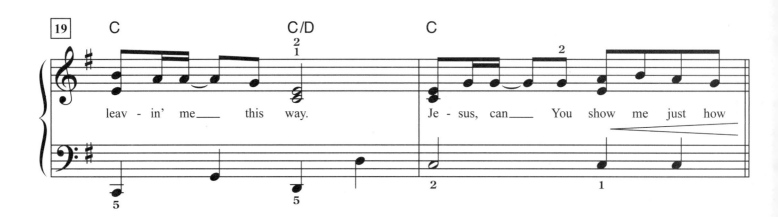

leav - in' me___ this way. Je - sus, can___ You show me just how

Chorus:

far the east is from the west? 'Cause I can't

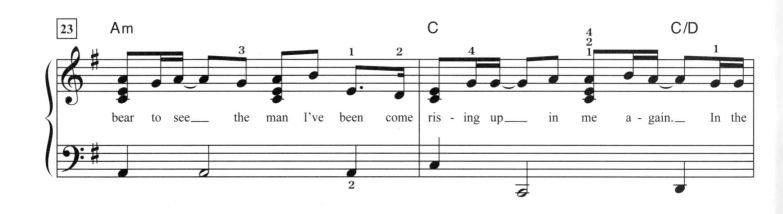

bear to see___ the man I've been come ris - ing up___ in me a - gain.___ In the

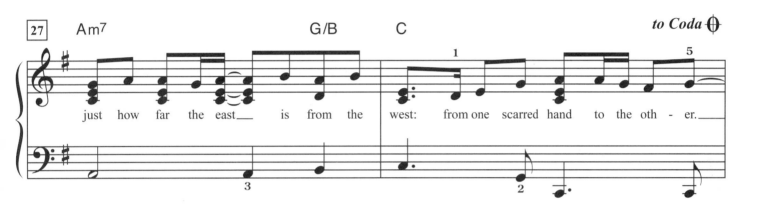

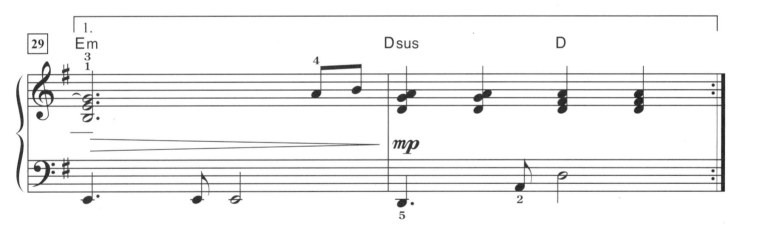

18

light. I need Your peace___ to get me through,___ to get me through___ this

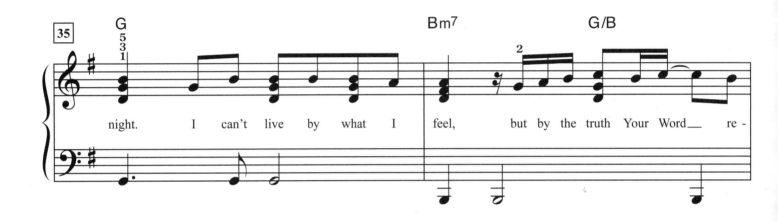

night. I can't live by what I feel, but by the truth Your Word___ re-

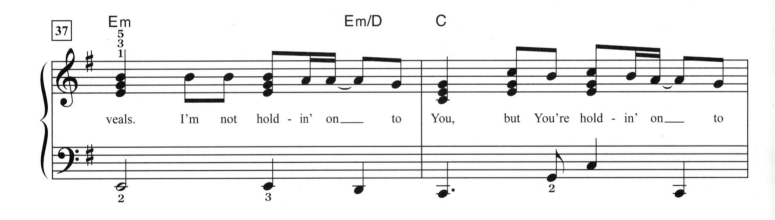

veals. I'm not hold - in' on___ to You, but You're hold - in' on___ to

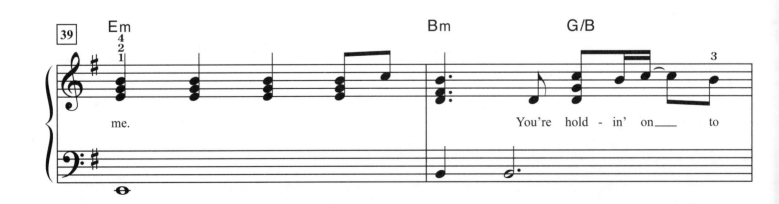

me. You're hold - in' on___ to

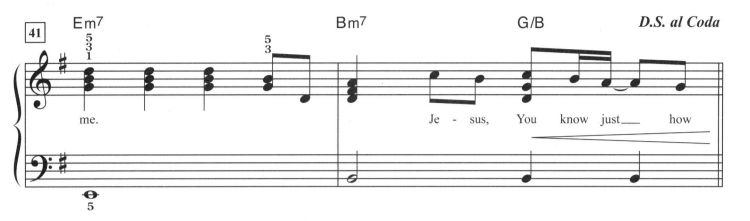

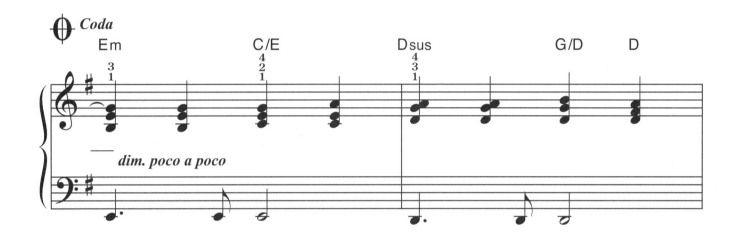

Verse 3:
I start the day, the war begins, endless reminding of my sin.
Time and time again Your truth is drowned out by the storm I'm in.
Today I feel like I'm just one mistake away from Your leavin' me this way.
(To Chorus:)

FREE TO BE ME

Words and Music by Francesca Battistelli
Arranged by Carol Tornquist

Verse 3:
Sometimes I believe that I can do anything,
Yet other times I think I've got nothing good to bring.
But You look at my heart and You tell me
That I've got all You seek, oh.
And it's easy to believe, even though
I've got a couple…
(To Chorus:)

GLORIOUS DAY

(Living He Loved Me)

Words and Music by
Mark Hall and Michael Bleecker
Arranged by Carol Tornquist

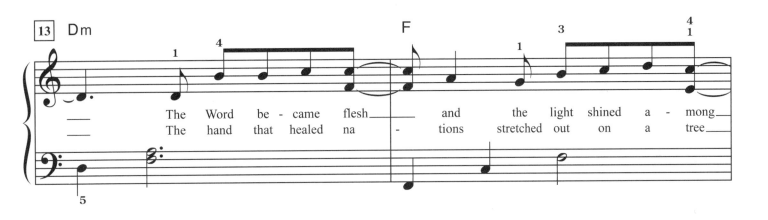

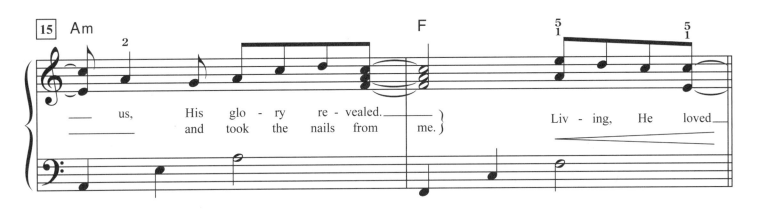

% *Chorus:*

Verse 3:
One day the grave could conceal Him no longer.
One day the stone rolled away from the door.
Then He arose, over death He had conquered.
Now is ascended, my Lord evermore.
Death could not hold Him; the grave could not keep Him from rising again.
(To Chorus:)

HE REIGNS

Words and Music by
Peter Furler and Steve Taylor
Arranged by Carol Tornquist

Verse 2:
Let it rise above the four winds, caught up in the heavenly sound.
Let praises echo from the towers of cathedrals to the faithful gathered underground.
Of all the songs sung from the dawn of creation, some were meant to persist.
Of all the bells rung from a thousand steeples, none rings truer than this:
(To Chorus:)

HOW GREAT IS OUR GOD

Words and Music by
Jesse Reeves, Chris Tomlin and Ed Cash
Arranged by Carol Tornquist

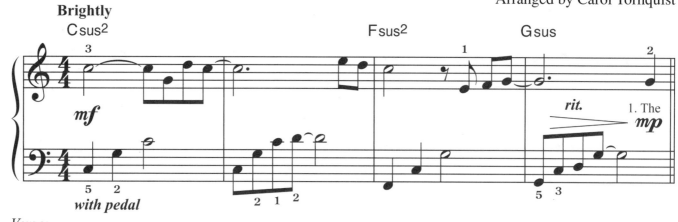

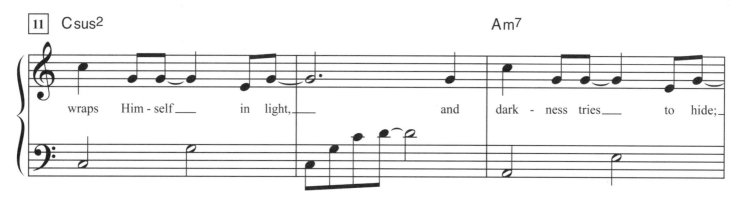

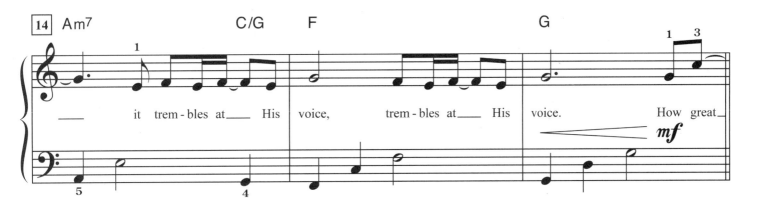

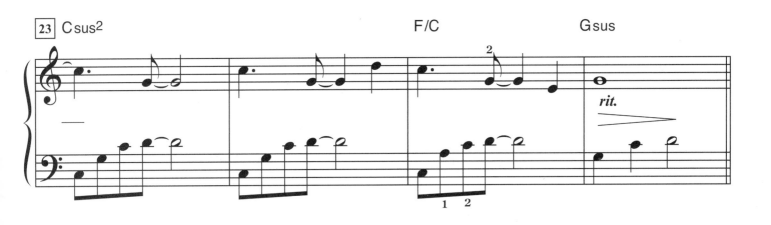

Verse:
a tempo

27 | Csus2 ——— Am7

2. Age to age___ He stands,___ and time is in___ His hands;___

30 | ——— F ——— G

___ Be - gin - ning and___ the End, Be - gin - ning and___ the End. The

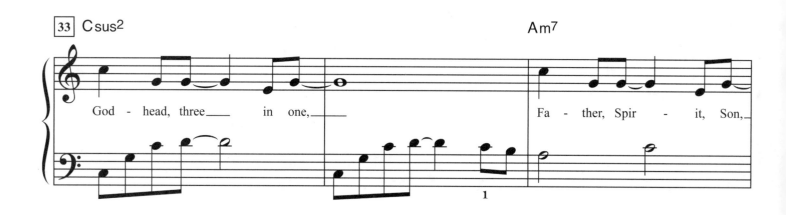

33 | Csus2 ——— Am7

God - head, three___ in one,___ Fa - ther, Spir - it, Son,

36 | C/G ——— F ——— Gsus

___ the Li - on and___ the Lamb, the Li - on and___ the Lamb. How great

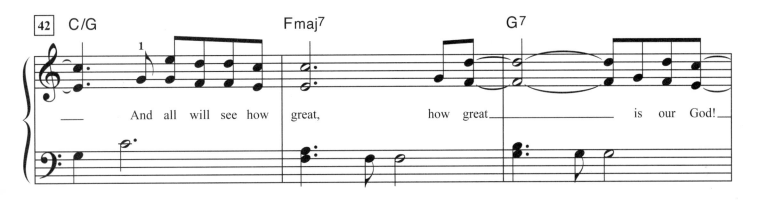

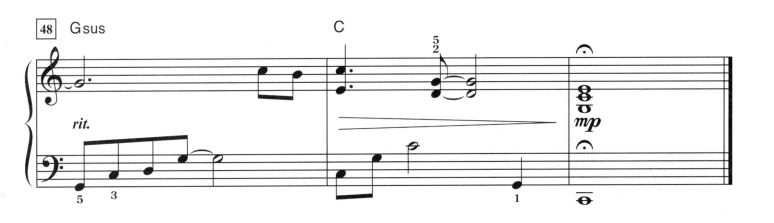

I WILL RISE

Words and Music by
Chris Tomlin, Jesse Reeves, Louie Giglio and Matt Maher
Arranged by Carol Tornquist

Moderately slow

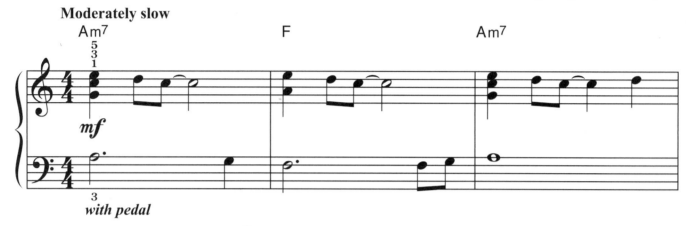

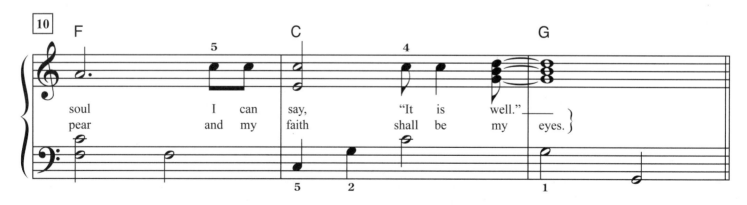

38

IN CHRIST ALONE

Words and Music by
Stuart Townend and Keith Getty
Arranged by Carol Tornquist

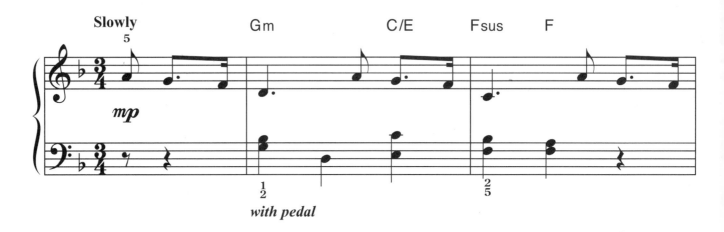

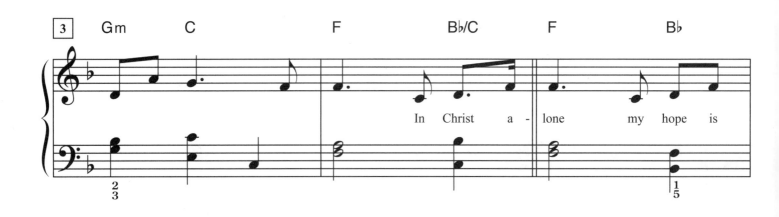

In Christ a - lone my hope is

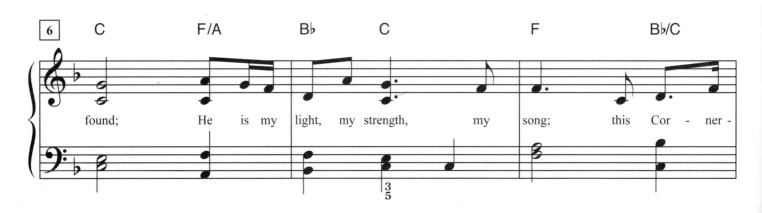

found; He is my light, my strength, my song; this Cor - ner-

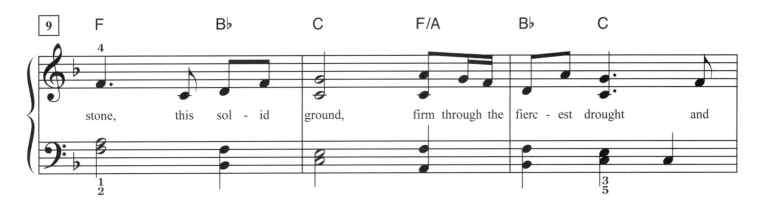

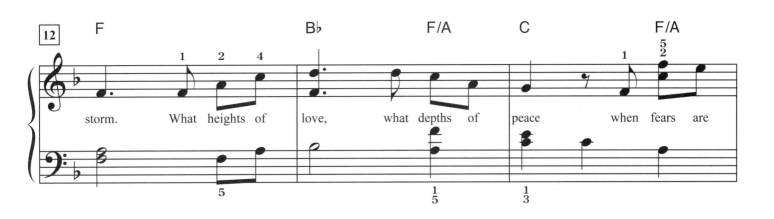

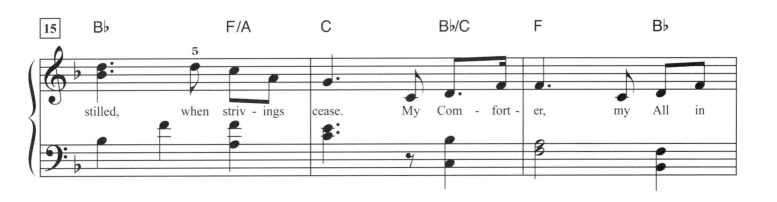

No guilt in life, no fear in death; this is the

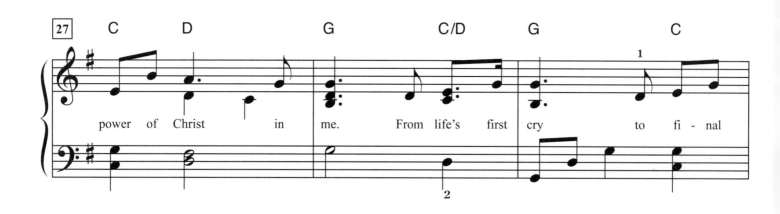

power of Christ in me. From life's first cry to fi - nal

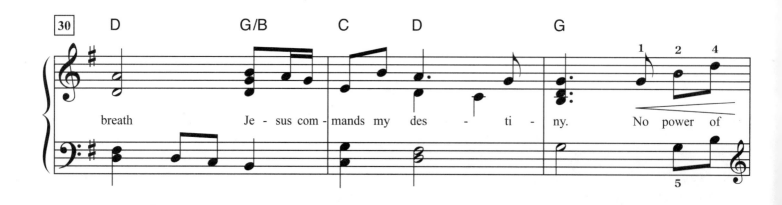

breath Je - sus com - mands my des - ti - ny. No power of

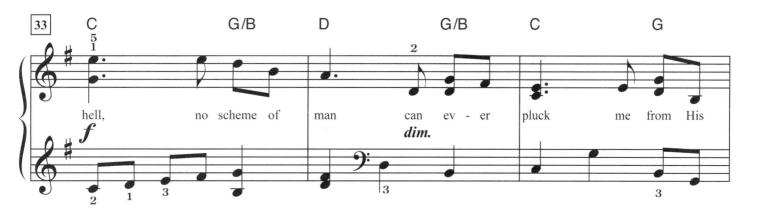

hell,   no scheme of man   can ev - er   pluck   me from His

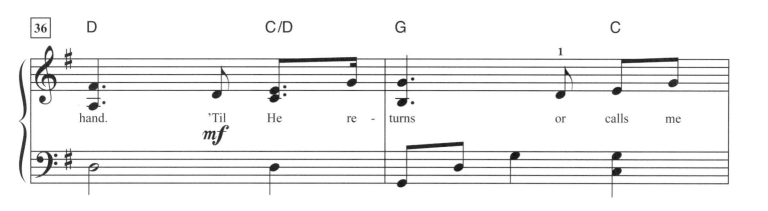

hand.   'Til He re - turns   or calls me

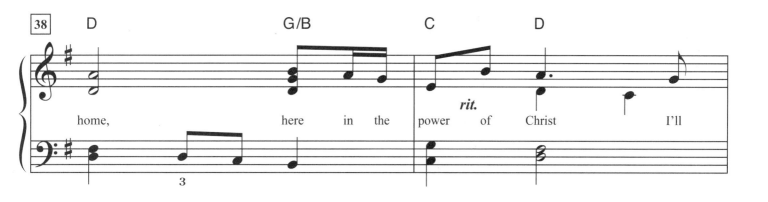

home,   here in the   power of Christ   I'll

Very slowly

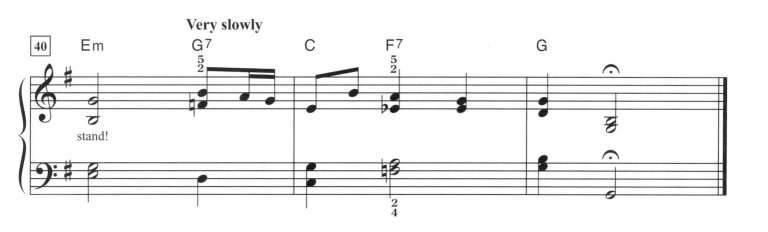

stand!

JESUS MESSIAH

Words and Music by
Daniel Carson, Chris Tomlin, Ed Cash and Jesse Reeves
Arranged by Carol Tornquist

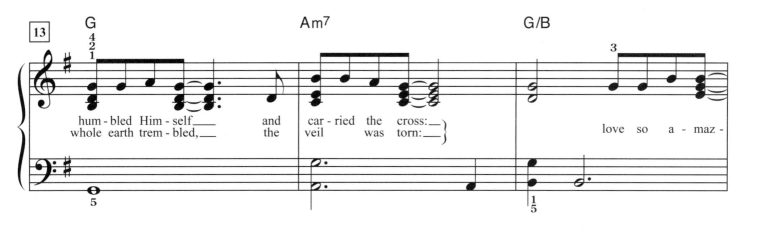

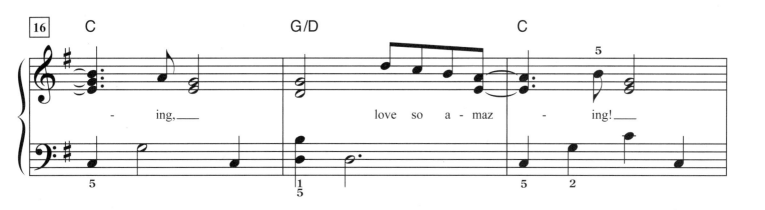

Chorus:

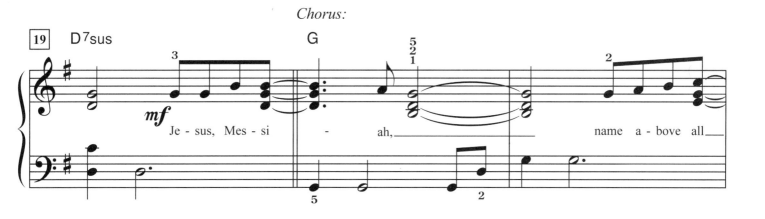

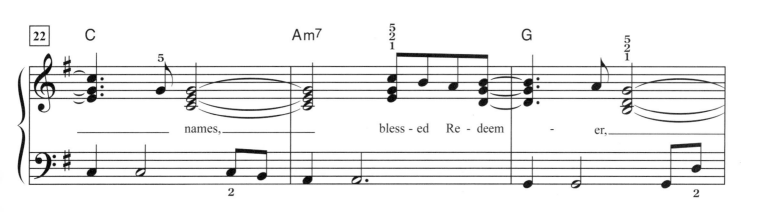

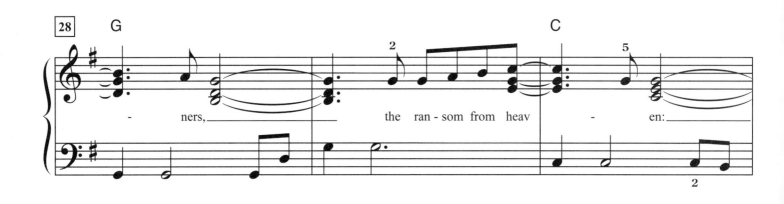

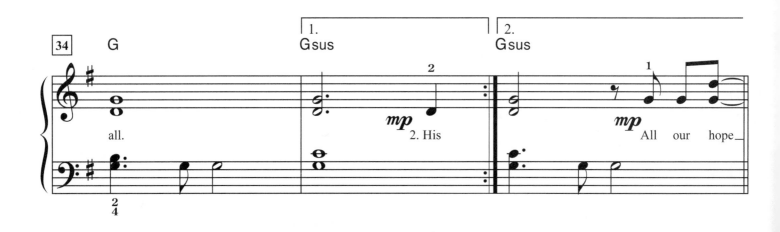

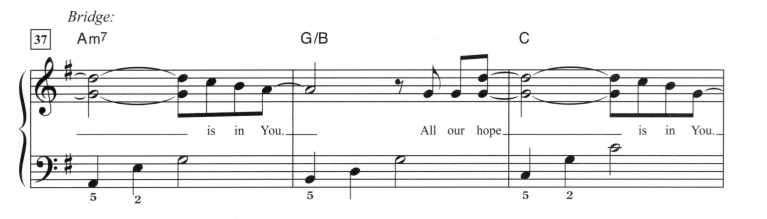

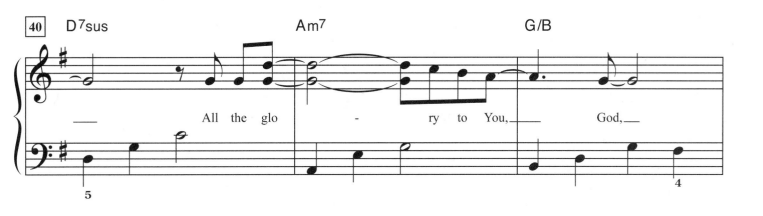

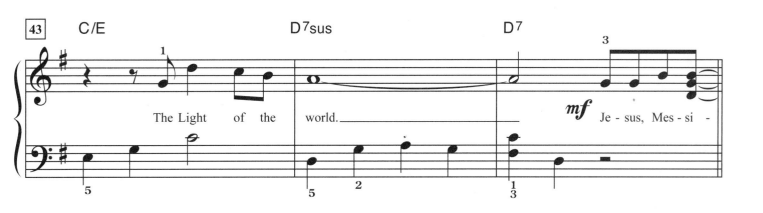

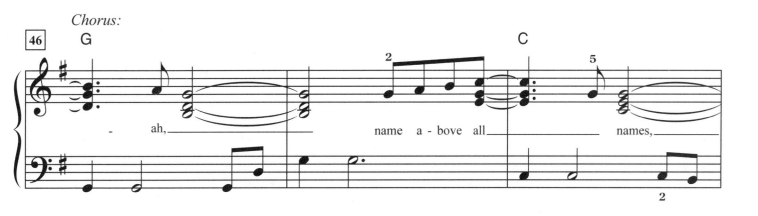

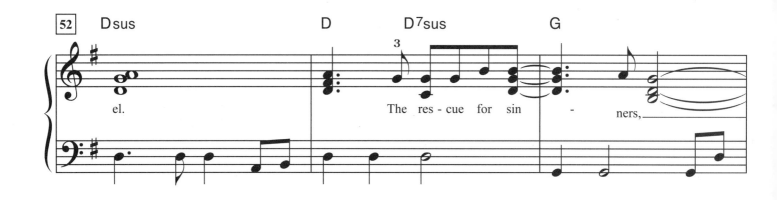

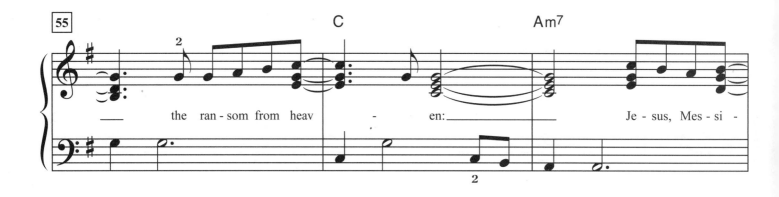

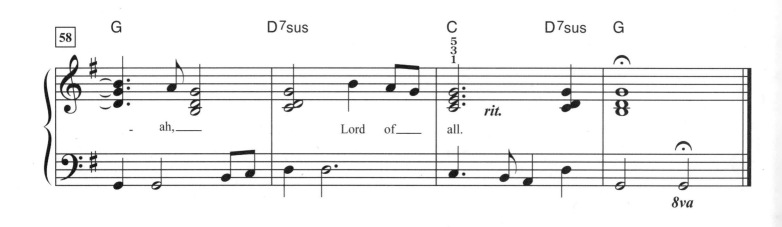

MY SAVIOR, MY GOD

Words and Music by
Aaron Shust and Dora Greenwell
Arranged by Carol Tornquist

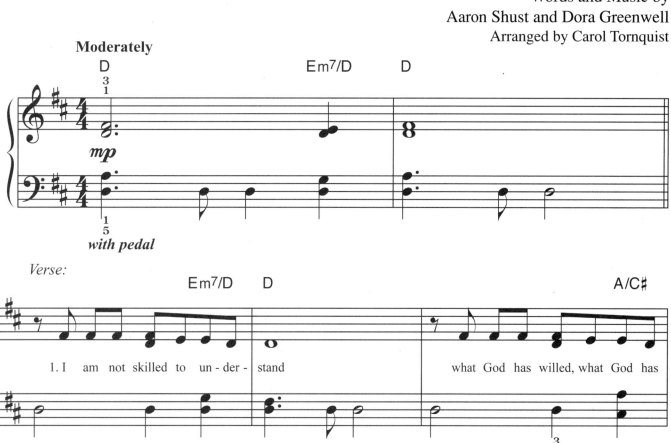

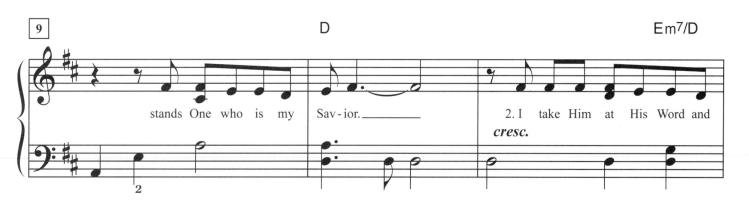

THE MOTIONS

Word and Music by
Matthew West, Samuel Mizell and Jason Houser
Arranged by Carol Tornquist

ONLY HOPE

Words and Music by Jonathan Foreman
Arranged by Carol Tornquist

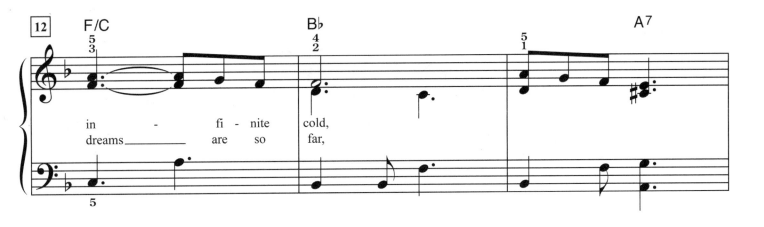

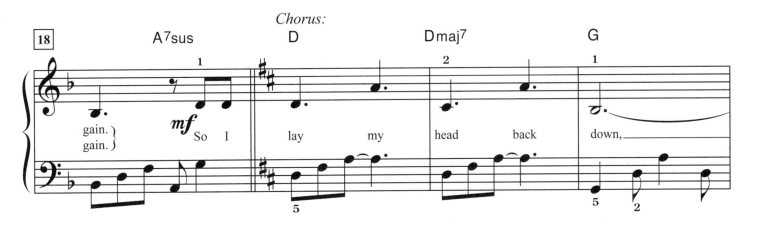

58

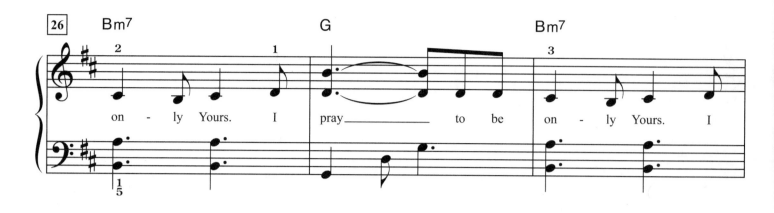

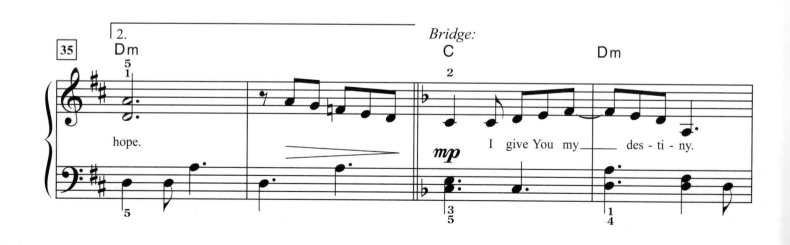

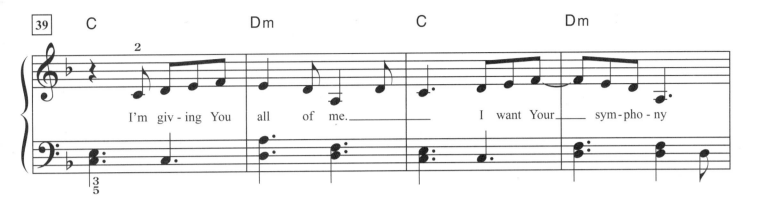

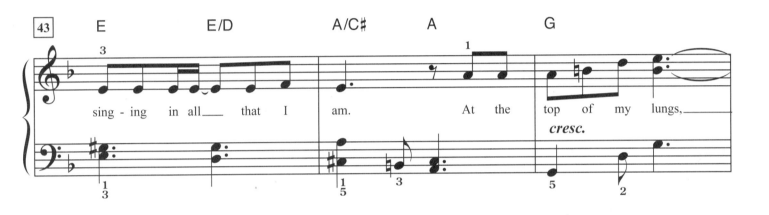

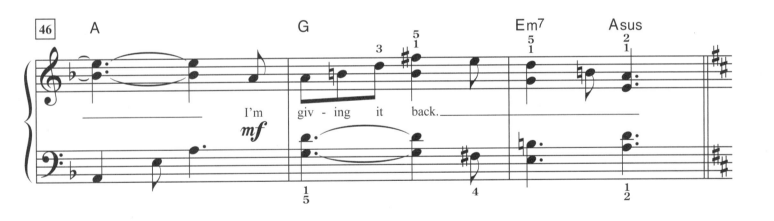

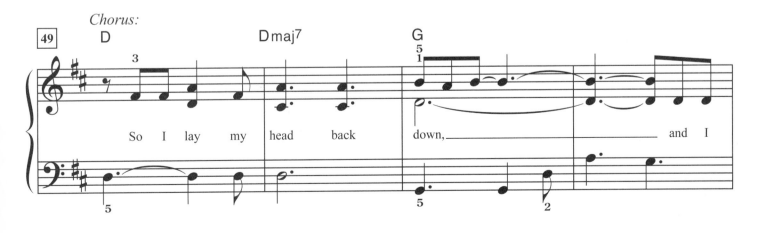

60

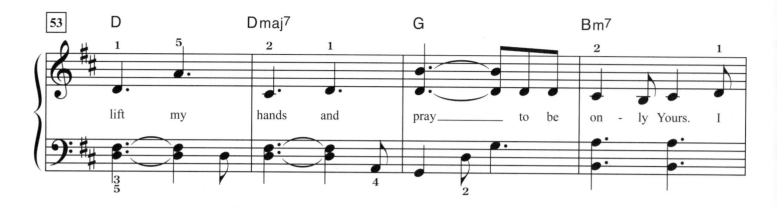

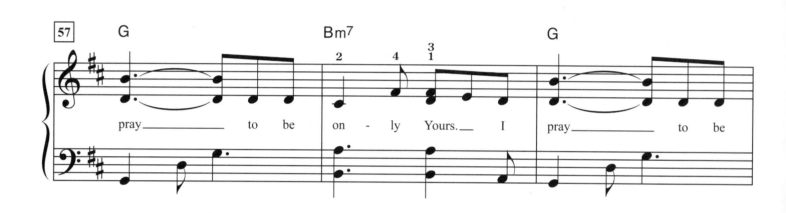

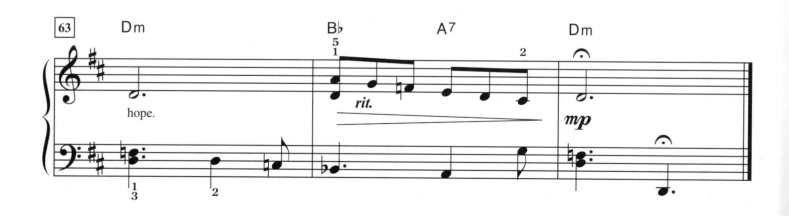

10,000 REASONS

(Bless the Lord)

Words and Music by
Matt Redman and Jonas Myrin
Arranged by Carol Tornquist

Verse:

1. The sun comes up, it's a new day dawn - ing.
2. You're rich in love and You're slow to an - ger. Your
3. *See additional lyrics.*

It's time to sing Your song ___ a - gain. ___ What - ev - er may ___ pass, and what -
name is great, and Your heart is kind. ___ For all Your good - ness, I will

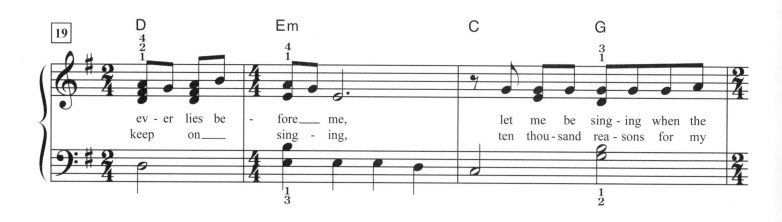

ev - er lies be - fore ___ me, let me be sing - ing when the
keep on ___ sing - ing, ten thou - sand rea - sons for my

eve - ning comes. Bless the
heart to find.

Verse 3:
And on that day when my strength is failing,
The end draws near and my time has come;
Still, my soul will sing Your praise unending,
Ten thousand years and then forevermore.

STRONG TOWER

Words and Music by
Aaron Sprinkle, Jon Micah Sumrall, Marc Byrd and Mark Lee
Arranged by Carol Tornquist

THERE WILL BE A DAY

Words and Music by Jeremy Camp
Arranged by Carol Tornquist

1. I try to hold__ on to this world with ev - 'ry - thing__ I
2. *See additional lyrics.*

have, but I feel the weight__ of what it brings, and the hurt that tries__ to

grab. The man - y trials that seem__ to nev - er end His Word de - clares__ this

Verse 2:
I know the journey seems so long, you feel you're walking on your own,
But there has never been a step where you've walked out all alone.
Troubled soul, don't lose your heart, 'cause joy and peace He brings;
And the beauty that's in store outweighs the hurt of life's sting.
But I hold on to this hope and the promise that He brings,
That there will be a place with no more suffering.
(To Chorus:)

UNTITLED HYMN

(Come to Jesus)

Words and Music by Chris Rice
Arranged by Carol Tornquist

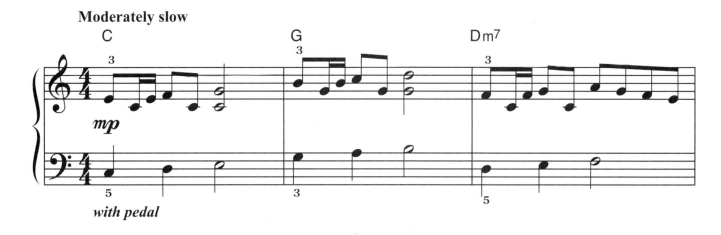

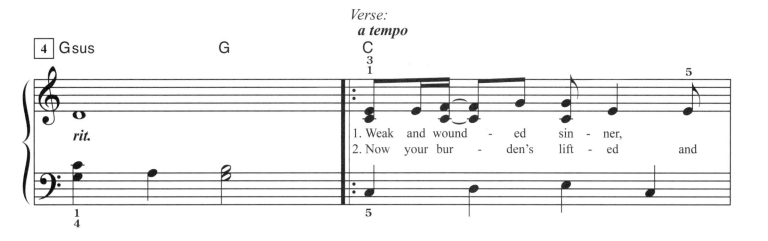

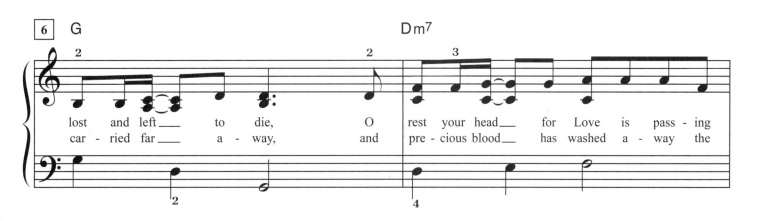

Chorus:

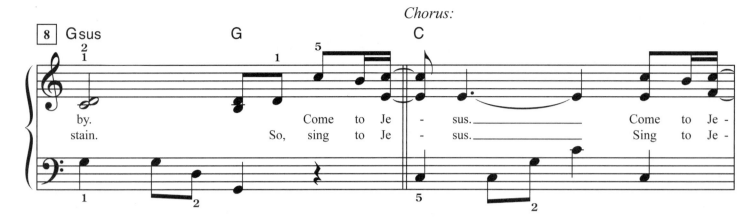

by.
stain.

Come to Je - sus._____ Come to Je -
So, sing to Je - sus._____ Sing to Je -

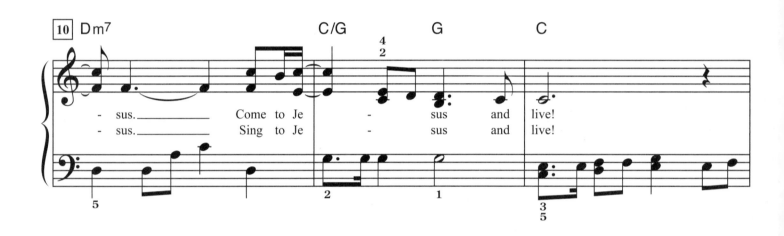

- sus._____ Come to Je - sus and live!
- sus._____ Sing to Je - sus and live!

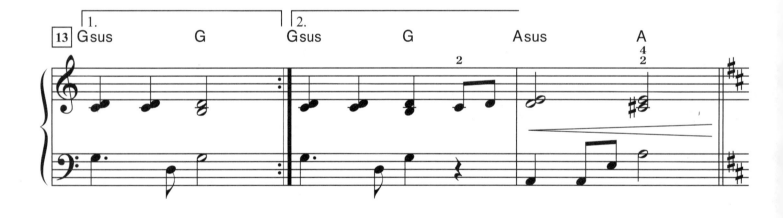

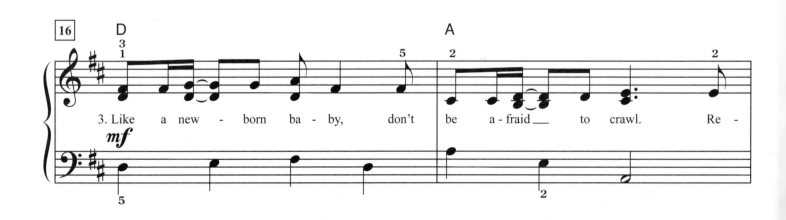

3. Like a new - born ba - by, don't be a - fraid___ to crawl. Re -

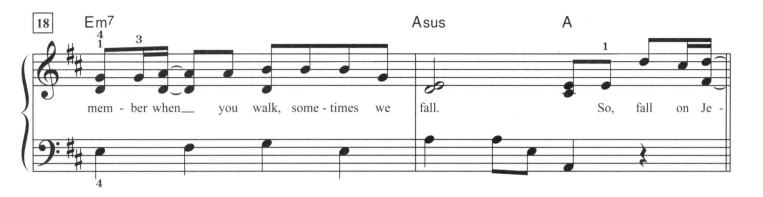

mem - ber when___ you walk, some - times we fall. So, fall on Je -

Chorus:

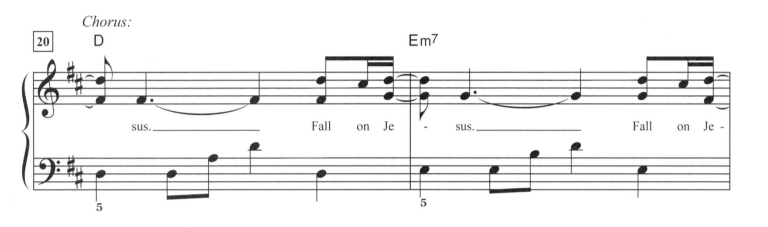

sus._____ Fall on Je - sus._____ Fall on Je -

sus and live!

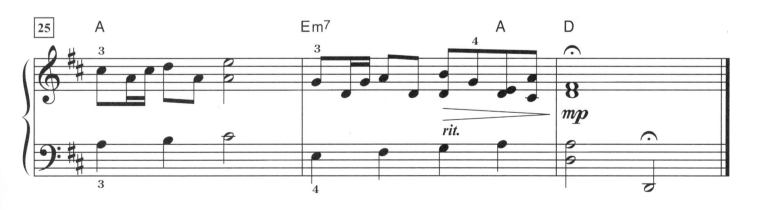

WORD OF GOD SPEAK

Words and Music by
Peter Kipley and Bart Millard
Arranged by Carol Tornquist

YOU RAISE ME UP

Words and Music by
Rolf Lovland and Brendan Graham
Arranged by Carol Tornquist

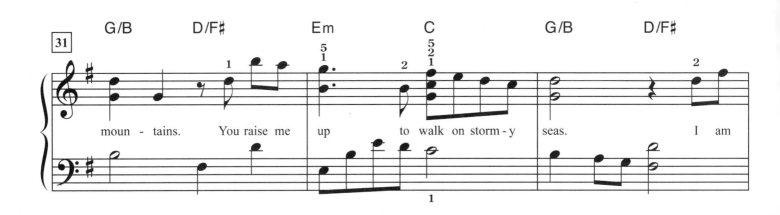

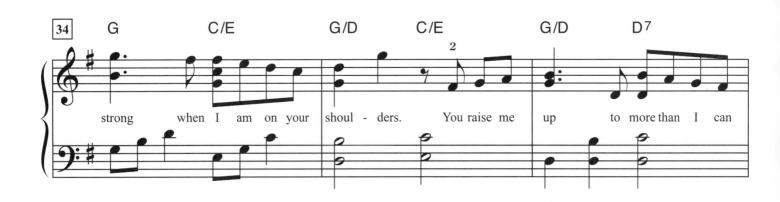

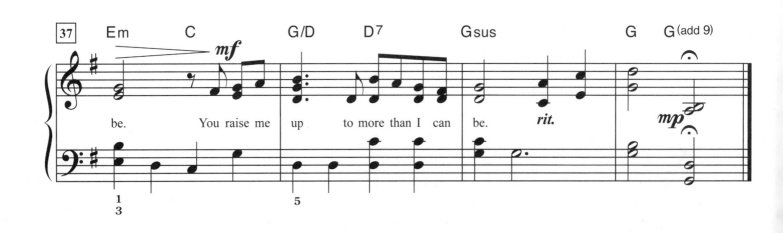